280051

Let's go by Train

Barbara Hunter

Heinemann
LIBRARY

Little Nippers

www.heinemann.co.uk/library
Visit our website to find out more information about **Heinemann Library** books.

To order:
☎ Phone 44 (0) 1865 888066
📄 Send a fax to 44 (0) 1865 314091
💻 Visit the Heinemann Bookshop at www.heinemann.co.uk/library to browse our catalogue and order online.

First published in Great Britain by Heinemann Library, Halley Court, Jordan Hill, Oxford OX2 8EJ, part of Harcourt Education.
Heinemann is a registered trademark of Harcourt Education Ltd.

Editorial: Jilly Attwood and Claire Throp
Design: Jo Hinton-Malivoire and bigtop, Bicester, UK
Models made by: Jo Brooker
Picture Research: Lodestone Publishing Limited
Production: Lorraine Warner

Originated by Dot Gradations
Printed and bound in China by South China Printing Company

ISBN 0 431 16462 2 (hardback)
06 05 04 03 02
10 9 8 7 6 5 4 3 2 1

ISBN 0 431 16467 3 (paperback)
06 05 04 03 02
10 9 8 7 6 5 4 3 2 1

British Library Cataloguing in Publication Data
Hunter, Barbara
Let's go by train
385.2'2
A full catalogue record for this book is available from the British Library.

Acknowledgements
The publishers would like to thank the following for permission to reproduce photographs:
Alvey and Towers p. **8-9**; Bubbles p. **7a** (John Howard), p. **18** (Jennie Woodcock); Eye Ubiquitous p. **4-5** (J. B. Pickering), **13a** (Bennett Dean); James Davis p. **20-21**; Popperfoto p. **10-11** (Michael A Nicholson); Sally and Richard Greenhill Photo Library p. **7b**; Sylvia Cordaiy Photo Library p. **16-17** (Nigel Rolstone); Tografox pp. **6**, **12**, **13b**, **14-15**, **19** (R. D. Battersby).

Cover photograph reproduced with permission of Eye Ubiquitous/J. B. Pickering.

The publishers would like to thank Annie Davy for her assistance in the preparation of this book.

Every effort has been made to contact copyright holders of any material reproduced in this book. Any omissions will be rectified in subsequent printings if notice is given to the publishers.

Contents

Journeys

Have you ever been on a train journey?

Many people go by train. They are called passengers.

Why do people go by train?

Work

Shopping

Holiday

There are places for you to sit and wait for your train.

Timetable

You need to look at a timetable to make sure you get the right train.

Departures

Depar

Time	11:17	Time	11:17	Time	11:17	Time		Time		Time	11:02		

Platform

PORTSMOUTH HARBOUR

Bus Service for Part of Journey

Please wait on this concourse

Calling at

East Croydon
GATWICK AIRPORT

Haywards Heath

Hove

Shoreham-by-Sea
Worthing

Barnham
Chichester

Southbourne

Emsworth
Havant Fratton

Portsmouth & Southsea
Portsmouth Harbour

Platform

LITTLEHAMPTON

via GATWICK APT

Please wait on this concourse

Calling at

East Croydon
GATWICK AIRPORT

Haywards Heath

Hove

Shoreham-by-Sea
Worthing

Durrington
Goring

Angmering
Littlehampton

Platform

Connecting Service

Please wait on this concourse

Calling at

Platform

Calling at

Don't forget your...

Evening Standard

Don't forget your...

Platform

Calling at

Don't forget your...

Evening Standard

Don't forget your...

Platform

BOGNOR REGIS

via GATWICK APT

Please wait on this concourse

Calling at

East Croydon
Purley

Redhill

Horley GATWICK AIRPORT
Three Bridges

Crawley

Horsham Christs Hospital
Billingshurst Pulborough

Amberley

Arundel

Ford Barnham
Bognor Regis

Change at Redhill for Reigate

10:48:17

ℹ **Customer Information**

Tickets ↘	13	GATWICK EXPRESS	14	Ti

Tickets

You have to buy a ticket before you get onto the train.

On the platform

You wait on the platform until the train stops. Then the doors open to let you get on.

Tracks

Trains travel on tracks.

Trains can go very fast. **Zoom!**

The train makes
a noise as it goes
over the tracks.

Jickety boom

Jickety boom

On board

Passengers can often buy food
and drinks on a train.

Old trains

Have you ever been on an old steam train?

Shapes

What shapes can you see on a train journey?

timetable

Travelcard

Valid only when shown with photocard no.

BKJ 7608

Class	Ticket type	Price
STD	SEVEN DAY	£61·00X RENEWAL 2333

Status

Valid until

20 JNR 02A 9324205230599

Between | Zones | Valid

HILDENBOROUGH * & R1256 ZONES 00M07D

Route/also available at

Valid within zone(s) indicated

ticket

tracks

Index

The end

Notes for adults

This series supports the young child's knowledge and understanding of their world and, in particular, their mathematical development. Mathematical language like *heavy/light, long/short*, and an introduction to different shapes and positional vocabulary such as *near/far*, make this series useful in developing mathematical skills. The following Early Learning Goals are relevant to the series:
• find out about, and identify, some features of living things, objects and events that they observe
• show an awareness of similarities in shapes in the environment
• observe and use positional language.

The series explores journeys and shows four different ways of travelling and so provides opportunities to compare and contrast them. Some of the words that may be new to them in **Let's Go By Train** are *arrival, departure, timetable, tickets, platform, loud speaker, tracks, electric* and *steam trains*. Since words are used in context in the book this should enable the young child to gradually incorporate them into their own vocabulary.

The following additional information about train journeys may be of interest:
The guard blows a whistle to show that it is safe for the train to leave the station. The train runs on tracks and points change the position of the tracks. There are signals and signs by the side of the tracks that the driver has to obey in just the same way as there are rules on the road.

Follow-up activities
The child could role play situations at a train station. Areas could be set up to create a ticket office, a platform and a train. Children who have been on a train may enjoy making a record of their journey by drawing, writing or tape recording their experiences to share with others.